Other Books by Jim Toomey

Sherman's Lagoon: Ate That, What's Next?

Poodle: The Other White Meat

An Illustrated Guide to Shark Etiquette

Another Day in Paradise

The 1992 to 1993 *Sherman's Lagoon* Collection
BY JIM TOOMEY

Andrews McMeel
Publishing

Kansas City · Sydney · London

Andrews McMeel Publishing, LLC
an Andrews McMeel Universal company
1130 Walnut Street, Kansas City, Missouri 64106

www.andrewsmcmeel.com

ISBN: 978-0-7407-2192-2

Library of Congress Control Number: 2001095894

Sherman's Lagoon may be viewed on the Internet at:
www.shermanslagoon.com

──────── **ATTENTION: SCHOOLS AND BUSINESSES** ────────

Andrews McMeel books are available at quantity discounts with bulk purchase for educational, business, or sales promotional use. For information, please e-mail the Andrews McMeel Publishing Special Sales Department: specialsales@amuniversal.com

To Valerie

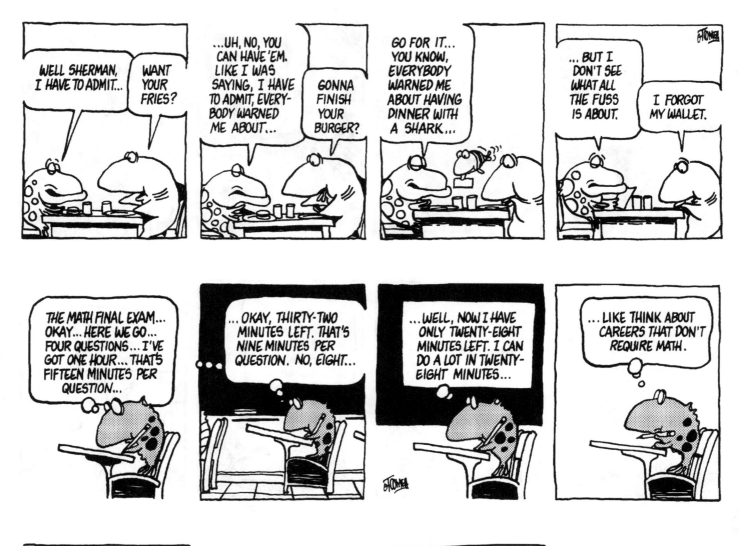

9

11

15

16

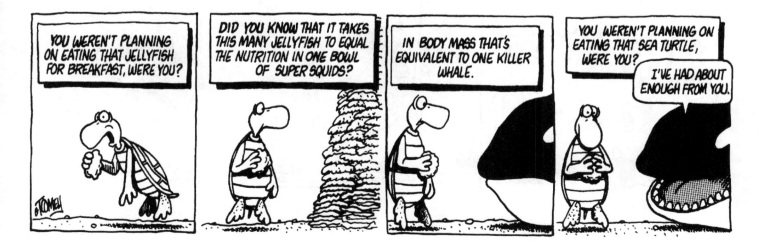

24

25

27

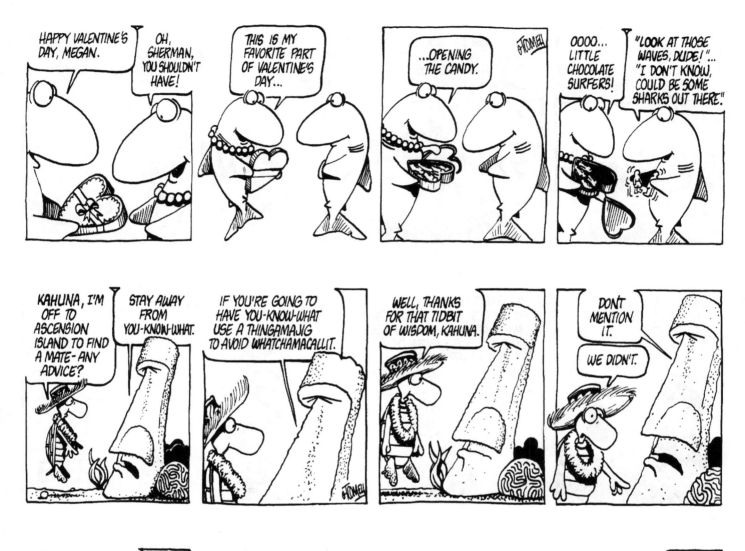

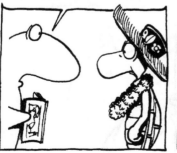

33

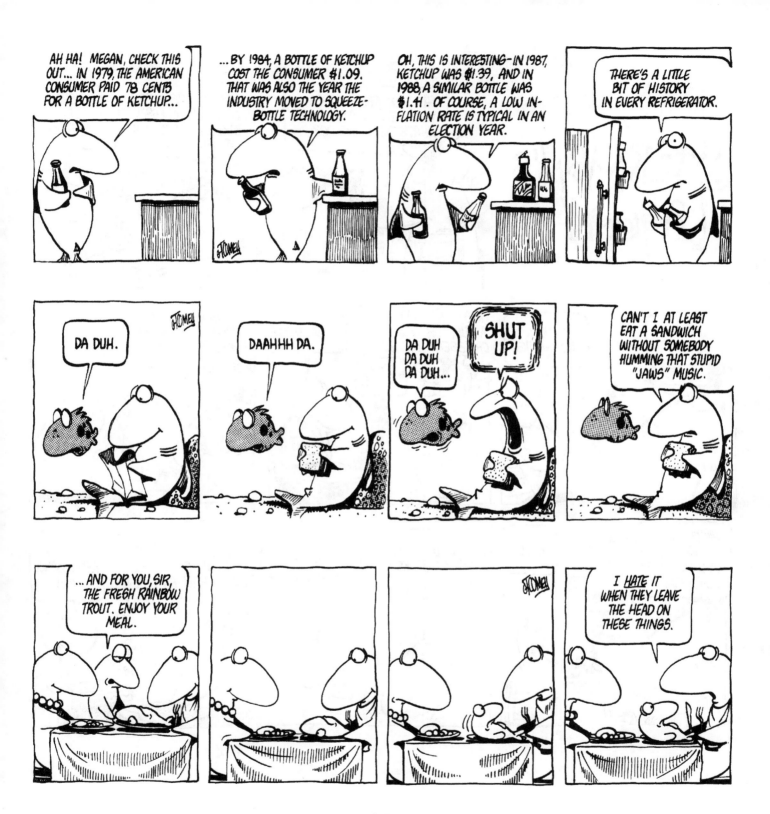

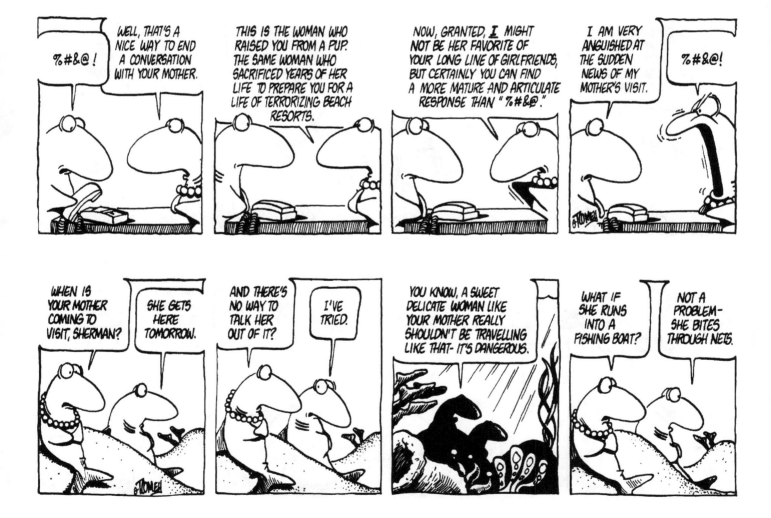

42

44

45

49

54

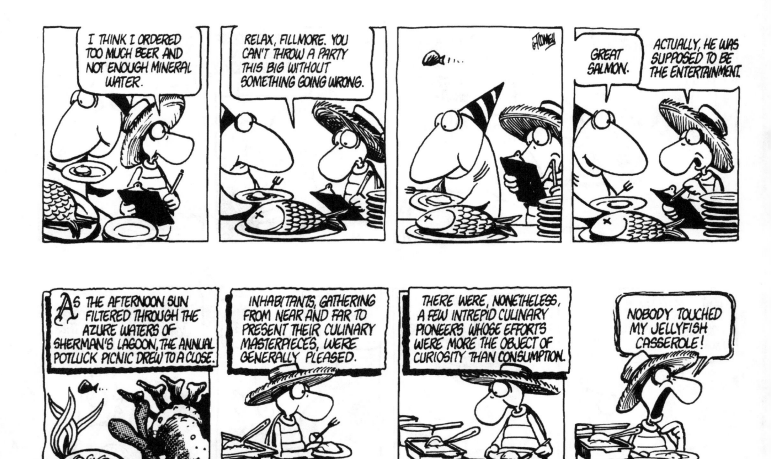

59

63

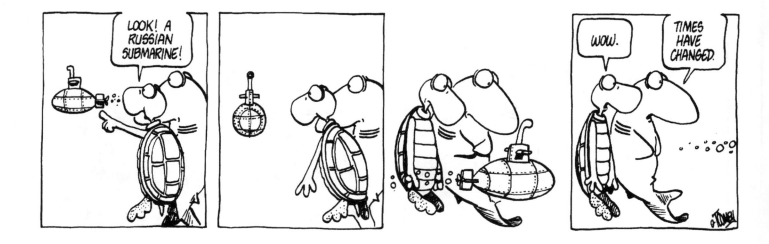

64

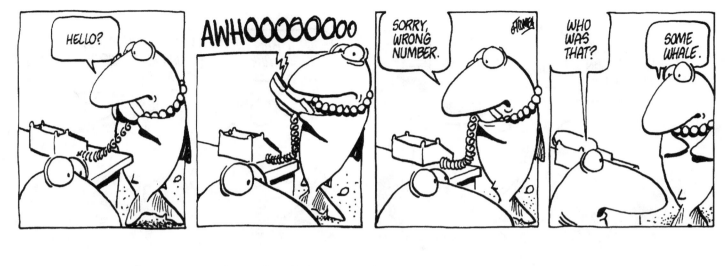

67

70

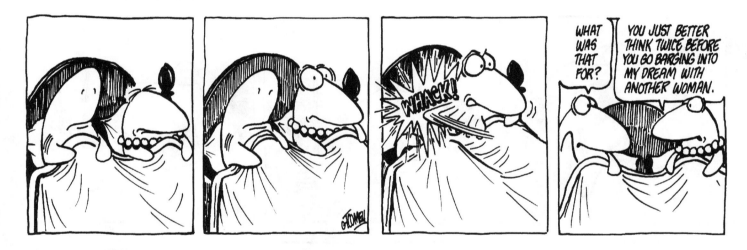

SHERMAN'S LAGOON

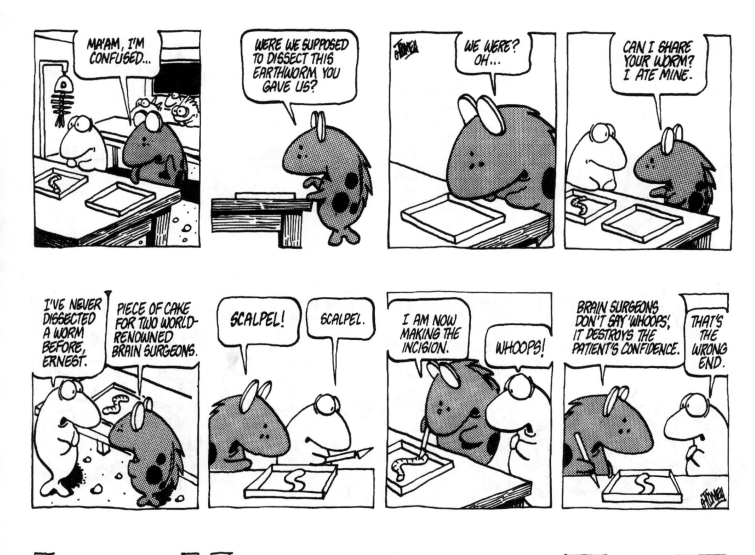

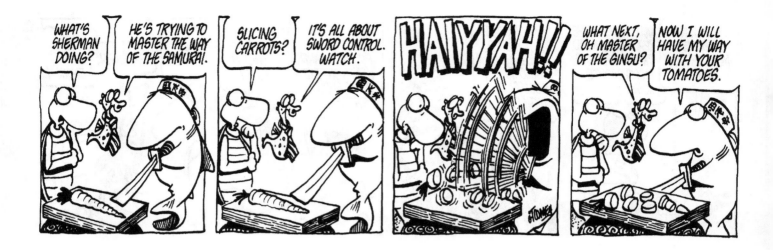

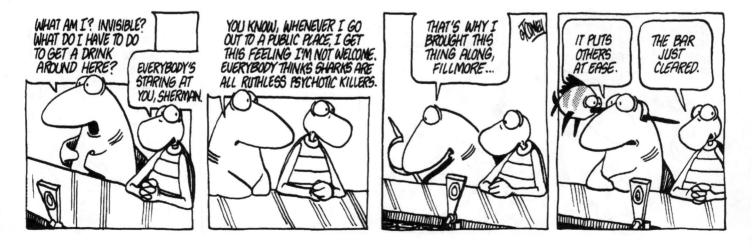

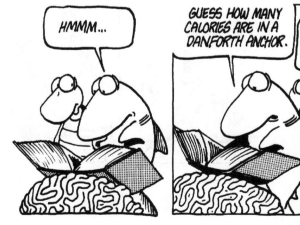

SHERMAN'S LAGOON

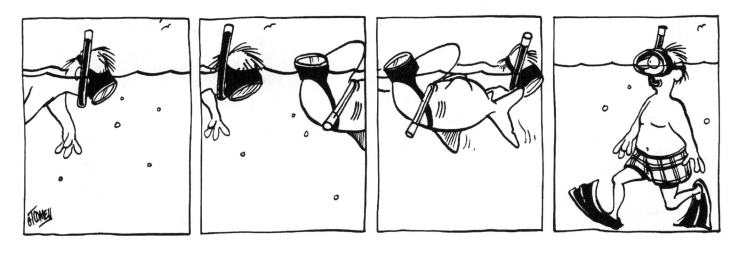

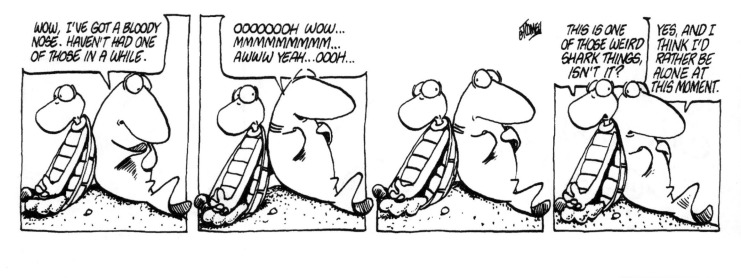

WOW, I'VE GOT A BLOODY NOSE. HAVEN'T HAD ONE OF THOSE IN A WHILE.

OOOOOOOH WOW... MMMMMMMMM... AWWW YEAH...OOOH...

THIS IS ONE OF THOSE WEIRD SHARK THINGS, ISN'T IT?

YES, AND I THINK I'D RATHER BE ALONE AT THIS MOMENT.

ERNEST, I WANT YOU TO LISTEN TO SOMETHING. THIS IS A SONG BY THE BEATLES THAT I USED TO PLAY EVERY DAY WHEN I WAS YOUR AGE.

THIS IS REAL MUSIC, ERNEST. IT'S NOT LIKE THAT NOISE YOU KIDS LISTEN TO NOWADAYS. THIS MUSIC HAD A PURPOSE.

BOY, MY PARENTS HATED THIS SONG.

PRECISELY.

I WANNA BE LOVED, BRODERICK.

IT'S MATING SEASON FOR YOU, ISN'T IT, FILLMORE?

I NEED SOMEONE WHO IS PASSIONATE. SOMEONE WHO LIGHTS UP IN MY PRESENCE.

EVERY SPRING YOU TURN INTO A HOPELESS ROMANTIC.

I WANT TO GO ON LONG WALKS ON THE BEACH AND ROLL AROUND IN THE SAND AND FROLIC IN THE SURF.

I WANT UNINHIBITED, UNCONDITIONAL, UNBRIDLED LOVE.

MAYBE YOU SHOULD GET A GOLDEN RETRIEVER.

SHERMAN'S LAGOON

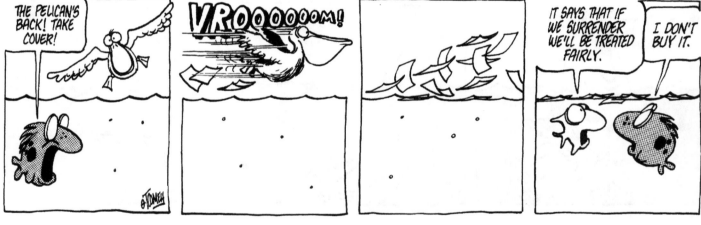

96

104

WE NEED A LONGER BUNGEE CORD.

106

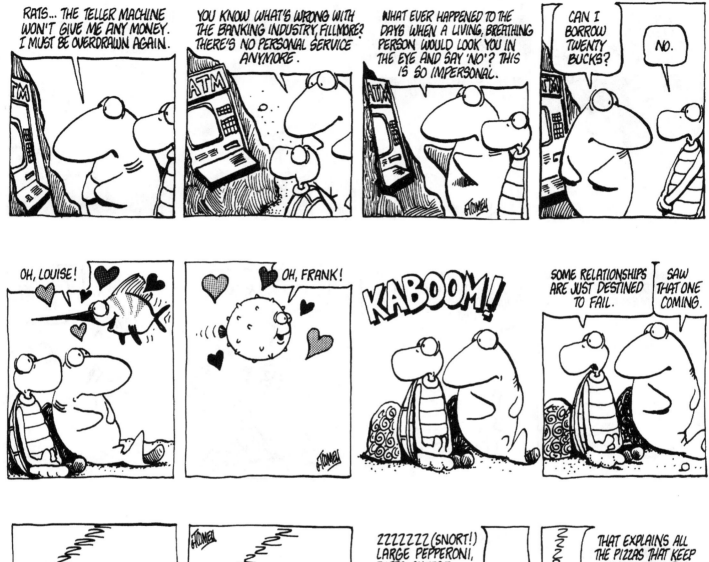

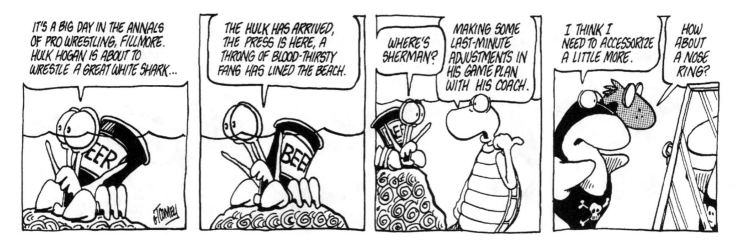

118

120

CPSIA information can be obtained
at www.ICGtesting.com
Printed in the USA
LVHW050836111020
668495LV00008B/884